The INSIDE & OUT GUIDE to
MIGHTY MACHINES

CLINT TWIST

THE INSIDE & OUT GUIDE TO MIGHTY MACHINES
was produced by

David West ☂ Children's Books
7 Princeton Court
55 Felsham Road
London SW15 1AZ

Designer: Gary Jeffrey
Illustrator: Alex Pang
Editor: Dominique Crowley
Picture Research: Victoria Cook
Consultant: William Moore

First published in the United States in 2006 by
Heinemann Library
a division of Reed Elsevier Inc.
Chicago, Illinois

Customer Service 888-454-2279
Visit our website at www.heinemannlibrary.com

11 10 09 08 07 06
10 9 8 7 6 5 4 3 2 1

Library of Congress Cataloging-in-Publication Data

Twist, Clint.
  The inside & out guide to mighty machines.
      p. cm.
  Includes index.
  ISBN-13: 978-1-4034-9087-2 (library binding - hardcover)
  ISBN-10: 1-4034-9087-2
  ISBN-13: 978-1-4034-9094-0 (pbk.)
  ISBN-10: 1-4034-9094-5
  1. Motor vehicles--Juvenile literature. I. Title. II. Title: Inside and out guide to mighty machines. III. Title: Mighty machines.
  TL147.T89 2007
  629.04'6--dc22

2006010936

Acknowledgements
The author and publisher are grateful to the following for permission to reproduce copyright material:
6t, Michal Wawruszak, 6b, Sierrarat; 7t, US Airforce; 8, exm company H Goussé; 9, exm company H Goussé; 10, Blue Angels US Airforce display team; 11t, Nicholas Koravos, 11b, US Airforce photo; 12, Northrop Grumman; 13, NASA; 15t, wikipedia.org, 15l, 15r, NASA; 17t, wikipedia.org, 17b, Lisa Morris, monsterphotos.co.uk courtesy of BIGFOOT4x4 Inc; 18, Sparwood Chamber of Commerce, Sparwood British Columbia; 19, Vasko Miokovic; 20t, Frans du Plessis, 20b, Michael Fuller; 23, Denver Public Library, Western History Collection, 0P-18453; 25t, 25b, US Department of Defence; 26, USS Nimitz photo lab; 27t, 27b, USS Nimitz photo lab; 29m, wikipedia.org

Every effort has been made to contact copyright holders of any material reproduced in this book.
Any omissions will be rectified in subsequent printings if notice is given to the publishers.

Printed and bound in China

The INSIDE & OUT GUIDE to
MIGHTY MACHINES

CLINT TWIST

Heinemann Library
Chicago, Illinois

CONTENTS

INTRODUCTION

STEP INSIDE THE AWESOME WORLD OF MIGHTY machines, and meet some of the toughest vehicles on Earth. From the rugged Abrams tank to the gritty monster truck, explore their strength and brawn both inside and out. Read about the technology that allows them to haul, lift, push and pull greater loads than ever before, as see-through artwork reveals the mechanisms behind their power.

SEA KING HELICOPTER

USED IN BOTH CIVILIAN AND MILITARY AIR-SEA OPERATIONS, THE MIGHTY Sea King and its crew of five brave all weathers to rescue people and ships in danger at sea.

The Sea King is a lifesaving helicopter. Two powerful Rolls-Royce Gnome engines spin five rotor blades, which fold up neatly when not in use. The ability to hover over a single spot allows the Sea King to lower its winch and winchman to hoist casualties to safety. Sea Kings played a vital role in the relief effort after the December 2004 Indian Ocean tsunami, delivering supplies and saving lives.

HEAVY METAL
Massive Russian Hind helicopters have as much firepower as a tank.

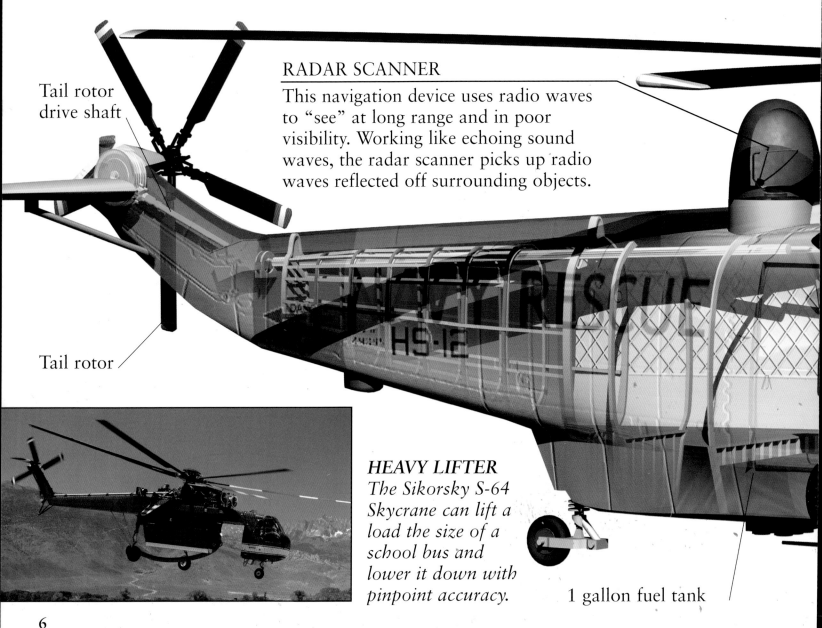

RADAR SCANNER

This navigation device uses radio waves to "see" at long range and in poor visibility. Working like echoing sound waves, the radar scanner picks up radio waves reflected off surrounding objects.

Tail rotor drive shaft

Tail rotor

HEAVY LIFTER
The Sikorsky S-64 Skycrane can lift a load the size of a school bus and lower it down with pinpoint accuracy.

1 gallon fuel tank

WESTLAND SEA KING (BASED ON SIKORSKY SH-3D)

SEA KING

Sea Kings were originally designed to attack enemy submarines. At first, they were equipped with missiles, depth charges, and air-launched torpedoes.

HYDRAULIC WINCH

About three people, or 600 lbs., can hang from the strong steel winch cable. Wind-induced swaying makes rescue hazardous. Including its crew, the Sea King can carry up to 20 people.

MAIN ROTOR

These long, flexible blades are made from a honeycomb of glass fiber and **carbon fiber**. They can withstand temperatures from – 40°F to 194°F and are strengthened by a strip of titanium.

TWIN JET ENGINES

If one of its two engines fails, a Sea King can travel up to 317 miles using the other. Sea Kings have a top speed of 155 mph.

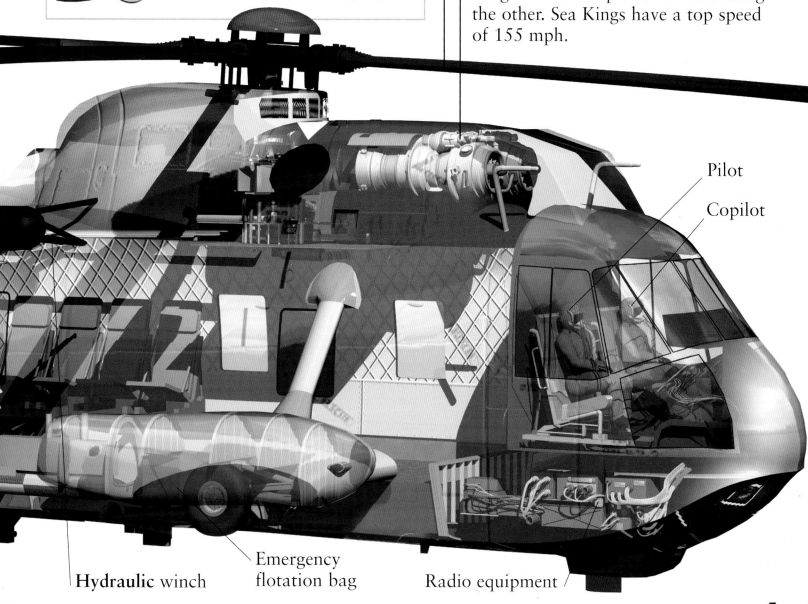

Pilot

Copilot

Hydraulic winch

Emergency flotation bag

Radio equipment

SUPER AIRBUS A380

THIS GIANT OF THE SKIES took fifteen years to develop. It carries 474 more passengers than a Boeing 747. The A380 storms down the runway at 169 mph and, once airborne, will cruise at 560 mph.

Hauling up to 555 passengers in a three-class layout, or up to 880 people in a single class, the enormous A380 is the world's biggest-ever commercial airliner. When fully laden and ready for takeoff, it weighs an astonishing 1,194,905 lbs.—about the same as 7,000 people. Within its spacious fuselage (cabin), a relaxation room, gym, and cocktail bar transform flying. Its parts are made separately in Germany, Great Britain, Spain, and France.

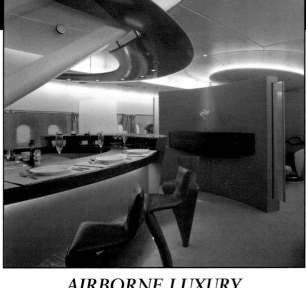

AIRBORNE LUXURY
Some airlines will include shops, a dining area, and even a casino on board A380s.

FLIGHT DECK

State-of-the-art instrument panels present the crew with detailed information. An electronic **autopilot** system can land the plane automatically.

Business class

Radar

First class

Nose wheel

Baggage hold

DOUBLE DECKER

Twin cabins extending along the aircraft's length accommodate 199 passengers on the upper deck and 356 on the lower deck.

Airbus claims that the environmentally friendly A380 will produce less noise and pollution than its closest competitor.

FOAM CONSTRUCTION

The fin is made of a honeycomb of plastic, reinforced by carbon fiber. It is lighter and stronger than material used on older planes.

Economy class

TURBOFAN JET ENGINE
Four huge turbofan engines, mounted on struts beneath the wings, produce enormous **thrust** (286,600 lbs.) to propel the A380 through the skies.

Engine exhaust

WING FUEL TANKS

Up to 82,000 gallons of fuel is stored in long fuel tanks inside the wings. This allows the A380 to fly nearly half-way around the world without refueling.

Control surfaces

Turbofan jet engine

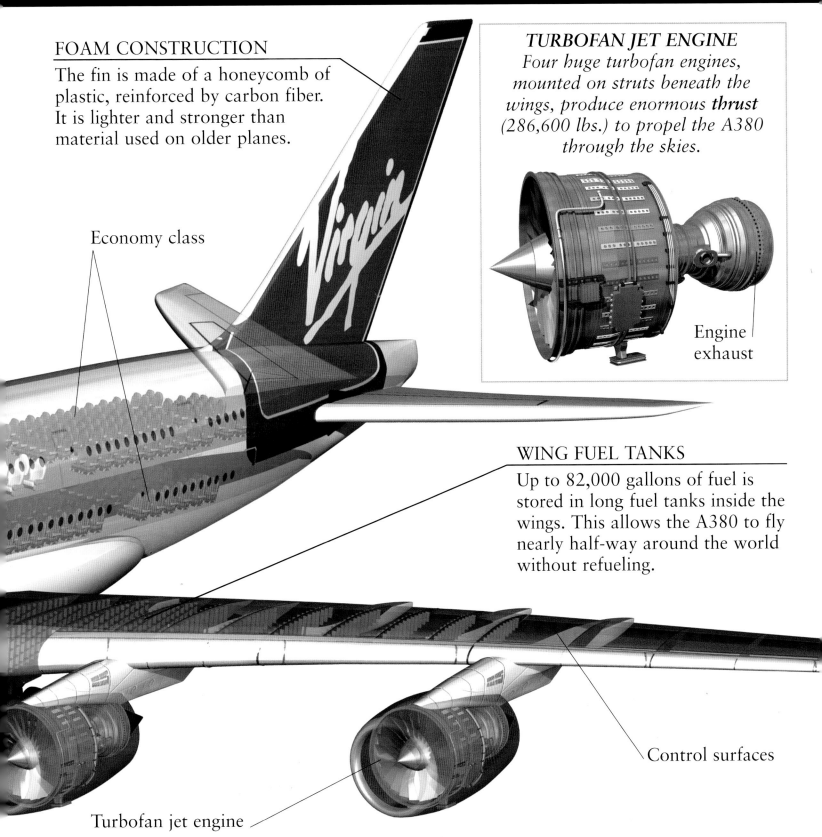

HERCULES

THIS MULTIPURPOSE AIRCRAFT IS THE MILITARY'S most versatile transport vehicle. Whether carrying fuel for air-to-air refueling, or flying tanks to a war zone, Hercules' fully pressurized cavernous fuselage can hold a varied range of cargo.

Sturdy Hercules are the longest-serving military aircraft, having flown for over 50 years. During this time, they have helped in civilian, military, and humanitarian aid operations. First designed in 1951 to transport 92 passengers, they are more often used to deliver cargo and supplies, and hold up to 67 tons (about 40 family cars). Access to the cargo hold is through the rear door, which can be lowered to form a full-width loading ramp. Hercules holds the world record for being the largest and heaviest plane to land on an aircraft carrier.

ROCKET BLASTOFF
When holding super-heavy loads, Hercules are fitted with solid fuel rocket boosters. These provide extra thrust at takeoff.

TURBOPROP ENGINE

Combining the power of a jet turbine (turbo) engine with the steady, long-haul performance of a **propeller** (prop) engine, the turboprop is strong, reliable, and durable.

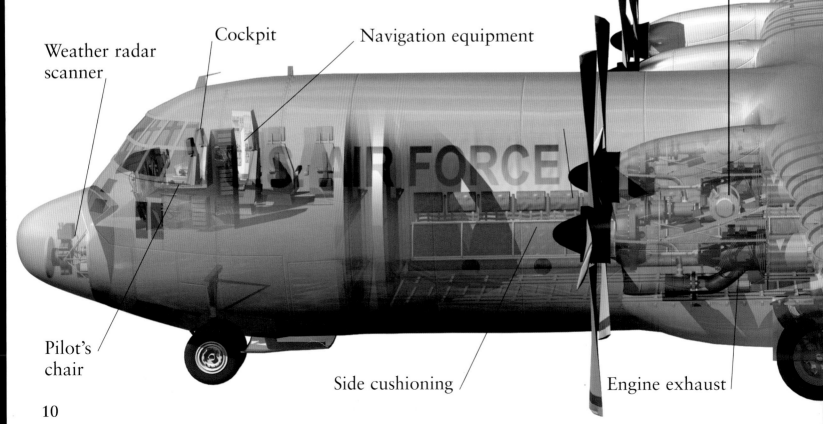

Weather radar scanner

Cockpit

Navigation equipment

Pilot's chair

Side cushioning

Engine exhaust

The Hercules is the world's most widely used STOL (short takeoff and landing) aircraft. It can deliver supplies to places with short runways, or none at all.

SURFACE SKIMMING
When Hercules release their cargo without landing, they lower the rear ramp and landing gear to increase air resistance. This helps slow down the plane to prevent goods from being damaged.

CARGO HOLD
Cargo is usually stacked neatly on wooden pallets and tied down with ropes and straps.

Wing-mounted
fuel tanks

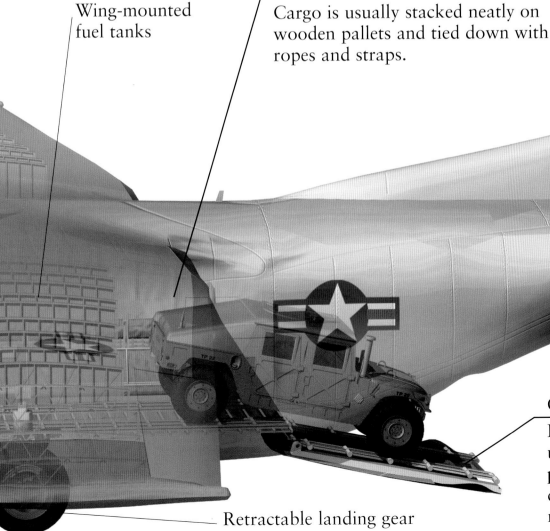

CARGO RAMP
For easy loading and unloading in midair, a **parachute** pulls cargo down and out off the ramp at the rear.

Retractable landing gear

11

B2 BOMBER

SILENT AND DEADLY, THE B2 IS A SUPER-advanced aircraft. Its top-secret stealth technology enables it to be invisible to radar, so it can drop bombs without warning. Its missions can last up to 48 hours, with refueling done in the air.

The B2 is the most costly aircraft ever developed. It would be cheaper to make it out of gold! A curved and zigzagged **bodywork** keeps it hidden from radar systems. When radar waves hit the plane, they bounce off in different directions, instead of straight back. Without the returning beams, a radar machine cannot tell there is a plane in the sky. Dark-colored antiradar paint also absorbs some of the waves to reduce the amount of radar reflected. Noise is muffled and heat insulated, making this stealthy plane almost impossible to detect and shoot down.

LATEST MODEL
The B2 (bottom) is the latest bomber aircraft to follow the more conventional shapes of the B1 (middle) and the B52 (top).

F118-GE-100 ENGINES

Hidden on top of the wing, these special engines cool the exhaust as it leaves the aircraft. This ensures that enemy systems cannot detect the B2 by using heat-detecting **infrared** devices.

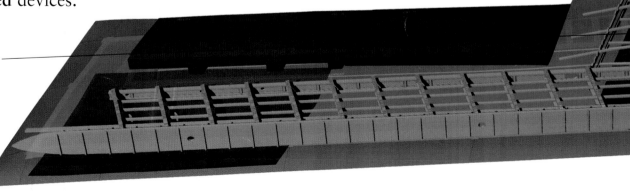

Air intake

Exhaust

Combustion chamber

Starboard outer fuel tank

NORTHROP GRUMMAN B2A SPIRIT

B2 STEALTH BOMBER

The B2 has a unique "flying wing" design—the tiny crew compartment is little more than a bump in the middle of the upper surface of the wing.

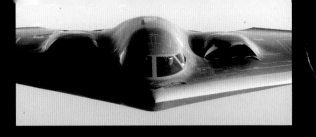

ROTARY BOMB LAUNCHER
Weapons are stowed away inside bays to prevent their detection by other military forces. A rotary launcher turns to release them one by one.

Bomb mounting clips

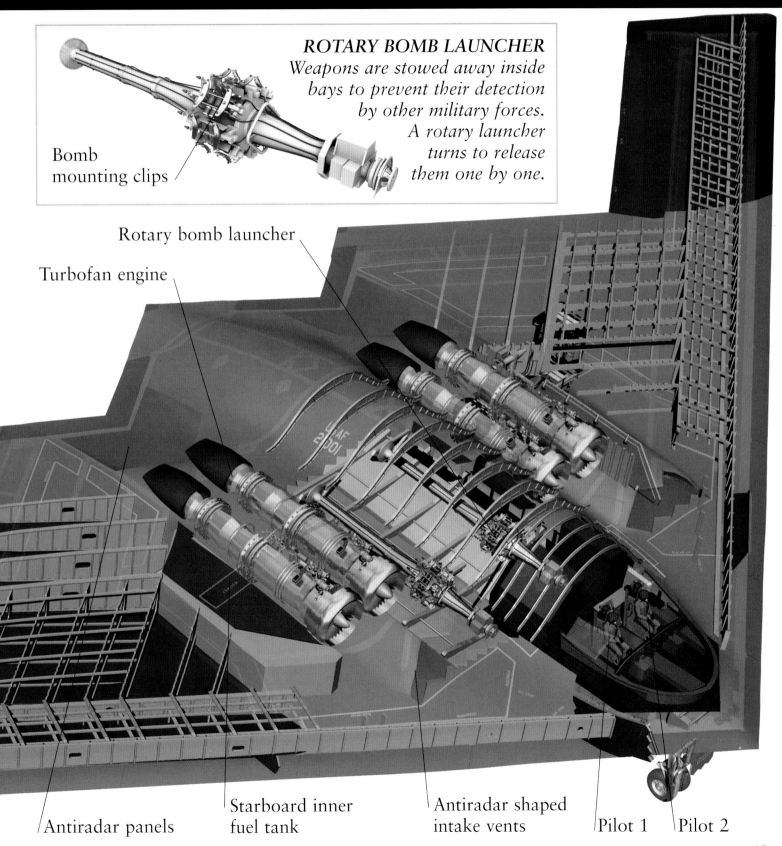

Rotary bomb launcher

Turbofan engine

Antiradar panels

Starboard inner fuel tank

Antiradar shaped intake vents

Pilot 1

Pilot 2

SATURN V ROCKET

BLASTING OFF FROM THE LAUNCH PAD, THIS MIGHTY rocket fired humans into their biggest adventure so far—the journey to the Moon.

Used in NASA's *Apollo* and *Skylab* programs, the *Saturn V* is the largest of the Saturn models. It is known as a triple-stage rocket because its three sets of engines are **ignited** consecutively to produce a giant force, called thrust, that shoots the rocket skyward. *Saturn V* is steered by its engines. There are five at the first stage. The middle one is fixed, and the other four turn to change the direction of travel. Once each section has burned its fuel, it is released from the rocket and falls away.

Second stage

Outer casing

First stage

Guidance fins

Saturn V rocket

OXIDIZER TANK

Fuel needs oxygen to burn. In space there is no oxygen, so *Saturn V* carries its own supply in order to burn fuel and propel itself.

FUEL TANK

The first-stage rocket engines use kerosene as fuel. Stages two and three use liquid hydrogen.

ROCKET ENGINES

Five F-1 rocket engines blast *Saturn V* from the launch pad. Fuel burns with the oxidizing agent inside reaction chambers. The hot streams of exhaust gases produced send the rocket soaring into the sky.

Wernher von Braun was a brilliant German rocket scientist. Following World War II, he designed the Saturn V *for the Americans and helped them to develop their space program.*

PAYLOAD SECTION
This is where the cargo is stored. It might be a spacecraft, an artificial satellite, or any number of astronauts. The payload can weigh up to thirteen tons.

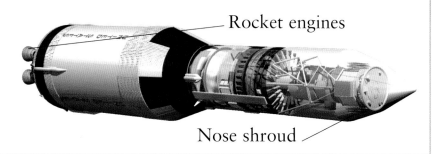

Rocket engines

Nose shroud

SKYLAB
In 1974, a *Saturn V* rocket launched the first space laboratory, which enabled astronauts to carry out experiments on their environment.

ALL SYSTEMS GO
Igniting on the launch pad, the first-stage F-1 engines blast the Saturn V *to 5,340 mph. They burn 2,200 tons of fuel.*

ORBITING LAB
Skylab remained in **orbit** *until 1979, when it fell back to Earth and burned up in the atmosphere.*

MONSTER TRUCK

THESE AWESOME VEHICLES started life as pickup trucks. Owners wanted to make them bigger and more powerful. An American named Bob Chandler stuck oversized tires on his Ford and started driving it over scrap cars. The Bigfoot trucks were born.

Crushing smaller vehicles with four gargantuan tires, monster trucks are the ultimate entertainment machines. An ultrastrong **suspension** system allows them to leap through the air and crash back to earth without damage. A **supercharger** boosts the engine's air intake, helping the fuel burn faster and produce more power. Occasionally, monster trucks run out of control and hurtle toward crowds of spectators. A **remote ignition interruptor** (RII) prevents fans from being injured by cutting out the engine to stop trucks from tearing away.

Shock absorber

ENGINE

A monster truck's vast V8 petrol engine provides a similar amount of power to that produced by a small tank. A **catalyst** speeds up the rate its immense engine burns fuel.

SUSPENSION

These enormous springs inside **pistons** absorb the vibrations created by landing heavily after a jump.

TIRES

Providing extra suspension, the huge tires provide grip, helping the monster truck clamber over **corrugated** surfaces or up steep and slippery hills.

16

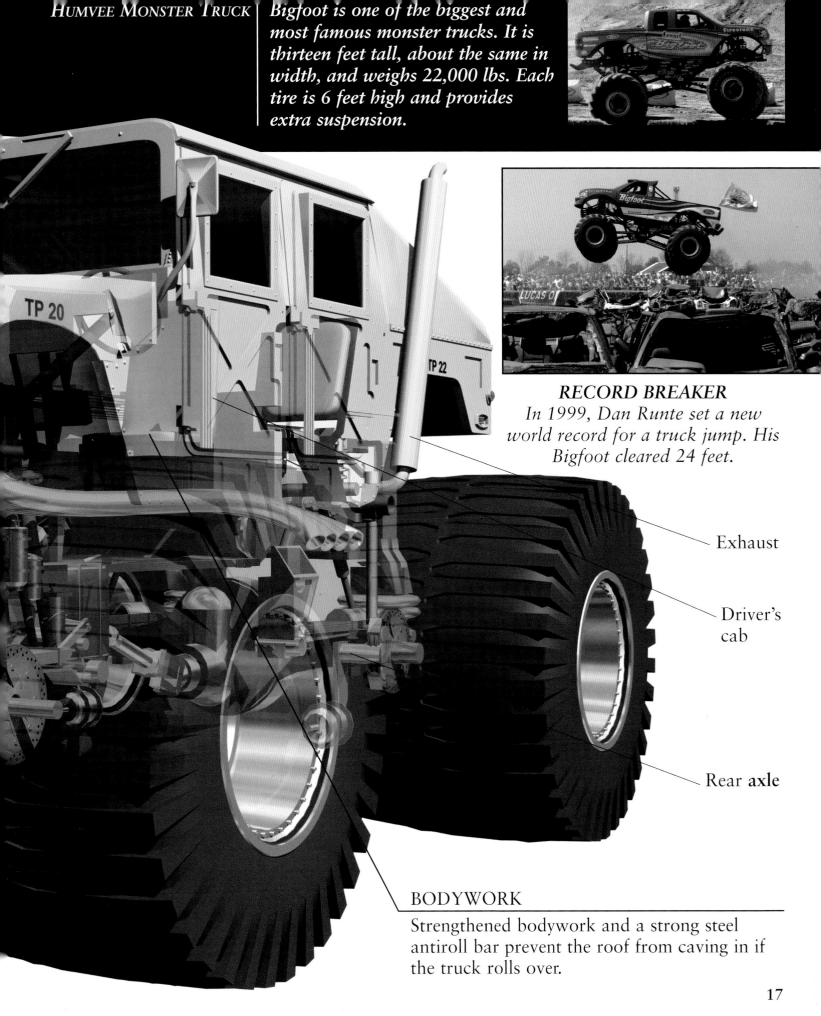

Bigfoot is one of the biggest and most famous monster trucks. It is thirteen feet tall, about the same in width, and weighs 22,000 lbs. Each tire is 6 feet high and provides extra suspension.

TP 20

TP 22

RECORD BREAKER
In 1999, Dan Runte set a new world record for a truck jump. His Bigfoot cleared 24 feet.

Exhaust

Driver's cab

Rear **axle**

BODYWORK
Strengthened bodywork and a strong steel antiroll bar prevent the roof from caving in if the truck rolls over.

GIANT DUMP TRUCK

No other truck matches the amazing carrying capacity of a giant dump truck. These are too huge to be driven on public roads, and are mainly used in the construction industry, in and around mines and quarries.

Hauling and dumping tons of debris, these giant transporters move loose material around construction sites. A V-shaped, reinforced tipping body is angled gently at the trucks' rear. This ensures that cargo slides out easily and causes minimal damage. Giant dump trucks have a short wheelbase (the distance between the front and rear wheels), which makes them very easy to maneuver, despite their enormous size and load. The tires are specifically designed to match a surface to reduce wear.

Tipping body

TIPPING POWER
The 777D delivers more than 100 tons of rock, the same weight as 1,000 people.

FINAL REDUCTION DRIVES
Fitted inside each wheel, these harness the power of the engine and concentrate it, to rotate the wheels steadily and slowly.

TIRES
Each of the six gigantic tires (four at the back and two at the front) measures nearly 9 feet in diameter—taller than a full grown man.

RETIRED DINOSAUR
The biggest giant dump truck ever was the Terex Titan, which could carry a load of more than 770,000 lbs.—the same as six Abrams tanks.

A fully laden Caterpillar 777D giant dump truck is the size of a two-story house. Even when empty, it weighs more than 100 family cars.

Hydraulic pistons

Tipping body

16-CYLINDER DIESEL ENGINE

With 16 cylinders, twice as many as a sports car has, the engine is super-powerful. It uses diesel fuel instead of gasoline because diesel engines have greater power to turn a wheel around an axis (torque) at lower speeds.

Suspension struts

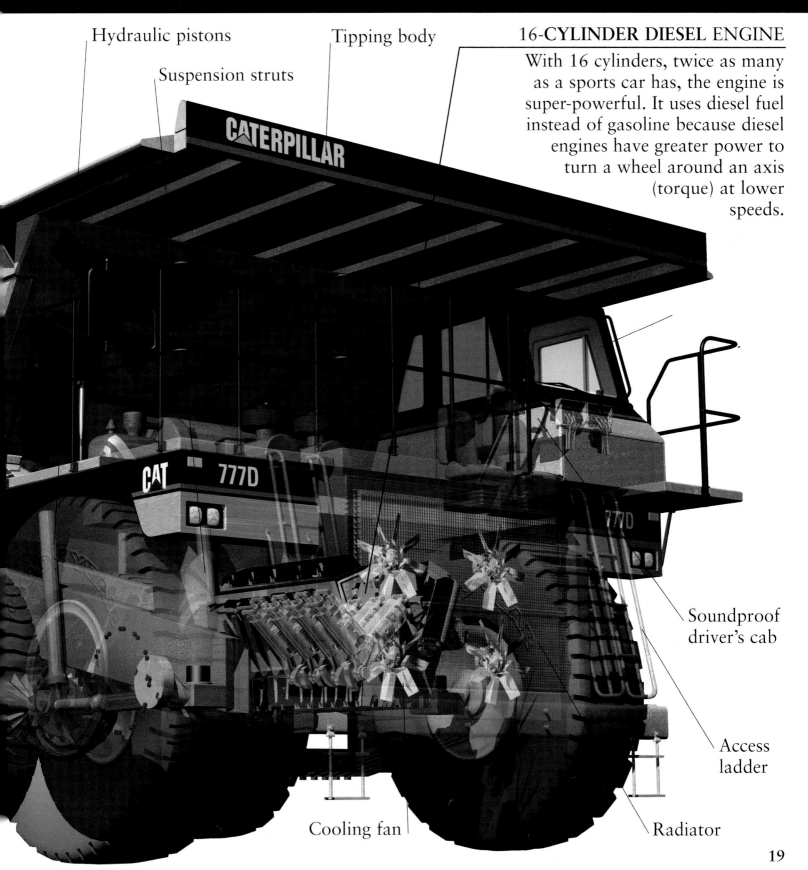

Soundproof driver's cab

Access ladder

Cooling fan

Radiator

19

BULLDOZER

FIGHTING FIRES AT OIL WELLS, CRASHING through forests, or demolishing small buildings, for sheer brute force and pushing power, nothing beats a bulldozer. Like the dump truck, these are found mainly on construction sites.

Originally a tractor adapted for construction and military use, the bulldozer tears down and scoops up everything in its path. Rock, trees, and soil are shoveled in "bull-dozes" or "giant measures" by the powerful dozer blade. Long, wide crawler tracks spread the pressure of 110 tons of machinery over a large area, preventing the bulldozer from sinking into soft ground. Special vehicles transport them, as they are too big to drive on roads.

SCRAPER
After the bulldozers have done the heavy work, grading machines are used to scrape the ground completely flat.

MINING SHOVEL
This giant mechanical shovel is used in quarries. It can rip away thousands of pounds of rock at a time and moves at walking speed, about 3 mph.

This bulldozer, trailing up a coal mountain, has two extra driving sprockets at the back. These transfer more power and give the tracks a triangular shape.

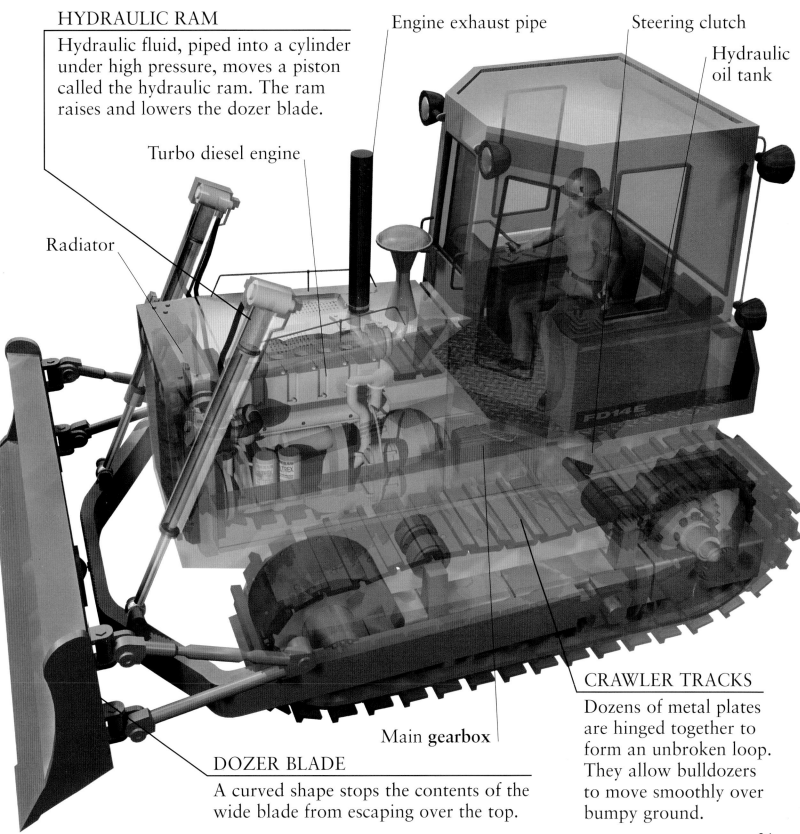

HYDRAULIC RAM

Hydraulic fluid, piped into a cylinder under high pressure, moves a piston called the hydraulic ram. The ram raises and lowers the dozer blade.

Engine exhaust pipe

Steering clutch

Hydraulic oil tank

Turbo diesel engine

Radiator

CRAWLER TRACKS

Dozens of metal plates are hinged together to form an unbroken loop. They allow bulldozers to move smoothly over bumpy ground.

Main **gearbox**

DOZER BLADE

A curved shape stops the contents of the wide blade from escaping over the top.

BIG BOY LOCOMOTIVE

Harnessing the power of steam to the fullest extent, Big Boy is the largest and most powerful steam locomotive ever built. It pulls heavier trains than any of its rivals, and is so long that its body must be hinged to curve around bends in the track.

Steam trains have been used for more than 150 years. They are powered by coal, which boils water to make steam. The steam is piped into cylinders that move pistons to turn wheels. Because the water is heated outside the cylinder, a steam engine is known as an external combustion engine. Gasoline and diesel engines produce heat inside the cylinders, and are known as internal combustion engines. Railway locomotives can only travel up gentle slopes because their steel wheels slide on steeper tracks.

BOILER
Water, held in dozens of long, narrow tubes, is heated here to make steam. Running at 40 mph, Big Boy turns 12,000 gallons of water into steam every hour.

FIREBOX
Coal is burned inside this box near the boiler. The firebox is usually made of steel or copper.

Driver's cab

TENDER
The tender is the storage area for large supplies of coal before it moves into the firebox, and for water before it becomes steam.

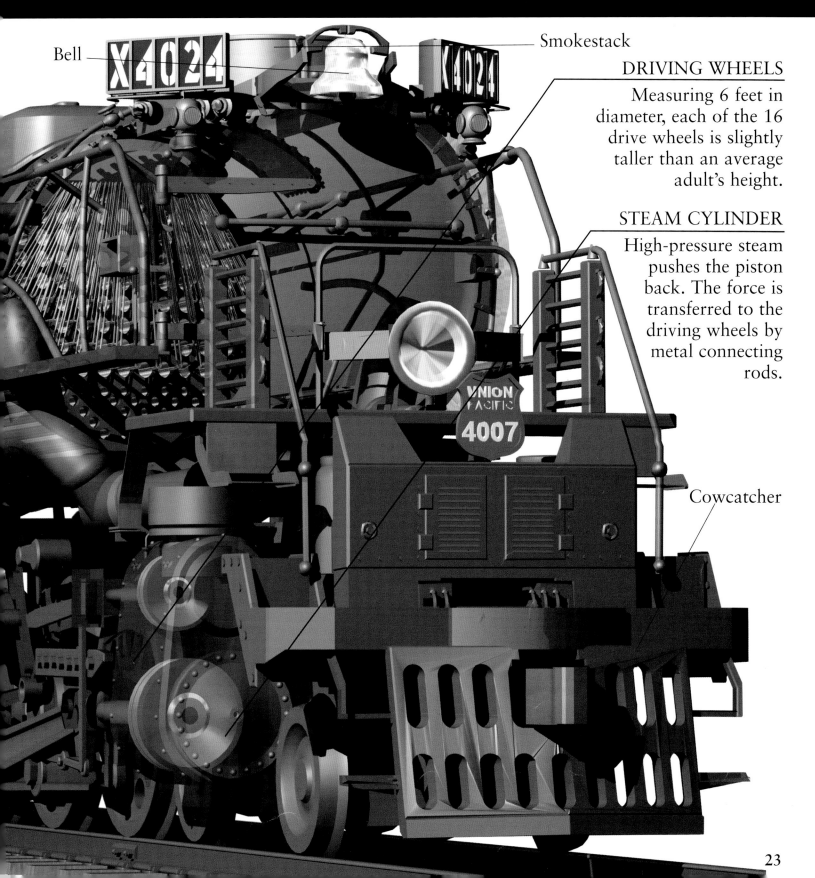

Big Boy was built to haul enormous freight trains across a mountainous region. It could pull a load of 6,600 tons along a slight uphill incline.

Bell

Smokestack

DRIVING WHEELS
Measuring 6 feet in diameter, each of the 16 drive wheels is slightly taller than an average adult's height.

STEAM CYLINDER
High-pressure steam pushes the piston back. The force is transferred to the driving wheels by metal connecting rods.

Cowcatcher

ABRAMS TANK

THE MOST ADVANCED TANK TO BE designed since World War II, the Abrams took more than a decade to develop. Invented in 1916, the first tank was a simple, lumbering gun platform. The Abrams has a powerful engine, excellent maneuverability, enormous firepower, and dense armor protection.

Weighing 68 tons, the Abrams is one of the heaviest tanks in the world. Yet, due to wide caterpillar tracks which spread its weight over a large area, it exerts less ground pressure per square foot than an average-sized van. The tank contains weak panels above its **ammunition** and reinforced walls between firearms and the crew. This ensures that if the tank is under fire and its ammunition ignites, it will explode away from the crew to keep them safe.

THERMAL VIEWER
Most objects produce heat. Thermal viewers sense heat and display it as a colorful image, to reveal an object even at night.

Armored side skirt

Ammunition compartment

GAS TURBINE ENGINE
This is a lightweight, powerful jet engine, like the ones used in an airplane. Expanding gases, from fuel burned in the combustion chamber, turn turbine blades attached to a central shaft. This provides enormous power to the drive wheels.

Designers made the Abrams as low as possible to make it a more difficult target. Sloping armor helps deflect bullets and shells fired by enemy tanks, protecting its four-person crew.

MAIN ARMOR

Layers of metals and other materials protect the Abrams from High Explosive Anti-Tank ammunition, known as HEAT rounds.

Smoke grenade launcher

MUZZLE BLAST

Controlled explosives launch special armor-piercing shells from the main gun, producing a bright cloud of smoke and hot gas around the gun's tip.

Driver's compartment

Mudguard

Track

120 MM GUN

The Abrams fires ammunition from its main gun at speeds of over 1 mile per second. It can destroy an enemy tank with a single shot and from more than 1.8 miles away.

Towing lug

Driver's station   Crawler tracks   Drive wheel

NIMITZ CARRIER

THIS HUGE WARSHIP contains over 193,750 square feet of flight deck and holds 80 modern combat aircraft. Measured from the keel (the bottom of the hull) to the tip of the mast, *Nimitz* is as high as an 18-story building.

USS Nimitz was named after Chester Nimitz, an Admiral in World War II. It carries high-speed strike aircraft that deliver bombs and rockets to distant targets. *Nimitz* also harbors jet fighters for defense against air attack, radar-equipped AWACs (early-warning aircraft), and helicopters for antisubmarine and search-and-rescue missions. Other weapons include missiles and multibarreled cannons. Beneath the flight decks, *Nimitz* is a small, self-contained city, criss-crossed by hundreds of passageways and staircases. Everything needed by the 5,680 person crew is crammed aboard—equipment, workshops, offices, storerooms, kitchens, a library, a barbershop, and a fully equipped, 53-bed hospital ward.

MIGHTY POWER
When fully loaded, weighing 95,000 tons, four five-bladed screws (propellers) drive Nimitz *through water at speeds of up to 36 knots (over 25 mph).*

Outgoing aircraft

CREW QUARTERS

Aircraft carriers operate 24 hours a day, seven days a week, and sailors work in shifts called "watches." At any given time, about one third of them will be off duty and asleep in their quarters.

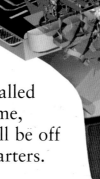

Nimitz is powered by a pair of Westinghouse A4W nuclear reactors. It could sail around the world many times without refueling.

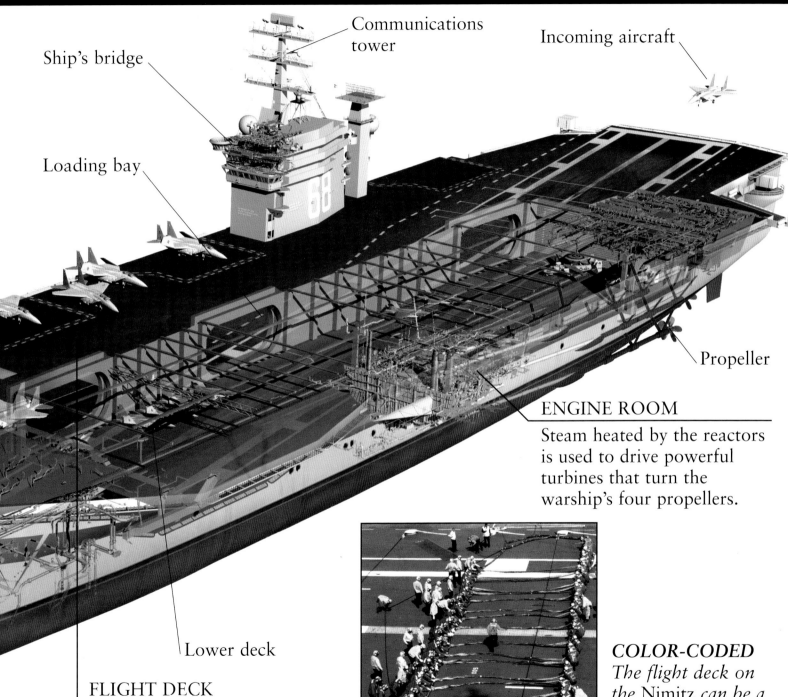

Ship's bridge

Communications tower

Incoming aircraft

Loading bay

Propeller

Lower deck

ENGINE ROOM
Steam heated by the reactors is used to drive powerful turbines that turn the warship's four propellers.

FLIGHT DECK
The flat upper deck is divided into two side-by-side runways so that two aircraft can take off at the same time, maximizing *Nimitz's* response to an enemy attack.

COLOR-CODED
The flight deck on the Nimitz *can be a dangerous place. To avoid confusion, each member of the deck team is color coded according to their role.*

TUGBOAT

FOR THEIR SIZE, TUGS ARE THE STRONGEST OF ALL boats. They are used mainly to guide ships into port, since very large vessels cannot manage small maneuvers. The most powerful tugs can keep a damaged oil tanker afloat, or haul up a sunken ship from the seabed, and can operate in the roughest conditions.

The *Nikolay Chiker* is the world's largest and most powerful tug. It measures almost 330 feet in length and can pull up to 275 tons. Strong steel lines, about 8 inches in diameter, are used to tow ships. Built in Finland in 1989, the *Nikolay Chiker* is a marine salvage tug, which means that it recovers either shipwrecks or their cargo, and sometimes both. It has a hospital on board, and a helipad, while its winches contain about 10 miles of cable, to pull up abandoned ships from the bottom of the ocean.

WATER PUMPS
The tug's pumps can move enough water to fill two Olympic-sized swimming pools per hour.

Bridge

HELIPAD
The helipad is the landing site for a helicopter, which might pick up casualties from a salvage operation who are in need of medical attention.

Anchor

Bow bulb

NIKOLAY CHIKER

DEEP SEA SALVAGE TUG

In a busy port, tugs are used to maneuver vessels in small spaces. They push against the side of the bow (front) or stern (back) to guide them to their berth.

CRANES

The *Nikolay Chiker* has three cranes, one on the starboard (right) side, and two on the **port** (left) side. They are used for hauling up objects from deep in the sea.

Crew cabins

TOWING

*Tugs can tow much larger structures than themselves, such as **oil-rigs**, bridge components, and even aircraft carriers.*

Rudder

DIESEL ENGINES

Up to four high-power diesel engines drive two propellers beneath the hull. The turning propellers shoot out jets of water behind the boat to push it along.

Thick steel hull

GLOSSARY

airborne
Flying in the air

ammunition
The bombs, shells, and bullets fired from a weapon

anchor
A heavy piece of metal with hooks, attached to a ship by a long metal chain. It catches on to objects on the seabed to keep a ship stationary.

autopilot
Short for automatic pilot, this machine steers the plane on a preset course

axle
A rod on which a wheel turns

berth
The place where a boat moors

bodywork
The outer shell of a vehicle

bow
The front of a boat

carbon fiber
A strong, light material that is used in airplanes and racing cars. It can be more than twice as stiff as steel.

catalyst
A substance that speeds up a chemical reaction without being changed

civilian
Any person who is not a member of the armed forces or police

corrugated
A surface made of a series of folded bumps, called ridges

cylinder
The metal sleeve inside which a piston moves

diesel
A type of fuel that burns when it is squashed, named after inventor Rudolph Diesel

gearbox
The box containing gears that transfer power from the engine to the wheels

hydraulic
Something that works by the pressure of water or another liquid in pipes

ignite
To set fire to

infrared
Radiation just beyond red in the visible spectrum. It is usually felt as heat.

nuclear reactor
A device that produces nuclear energy. Nuclear energy is the energy that exists in the center of tiny particles called atoms.

oil rig
The structure, machinery, and drilling equipment that are used to drill for oil

orbit
A circular path around a body in space, such as the Earth

parachute
A loose umbrella of light fabric used to slow things down in air

piston
A cylinder that moves to and fro within another cylinder

port
The term used to describe the left of a ship or aircraft

propeller
A device with a number of angled blades that spins to push water or air in a particular direction to move a boat through water or a plane through air

remote ignition interruptor
The RII enables an engine to be switched off from outside a vehicle

sprocket
A wheel with a set of teeth around its rim

starboard
The term used to describe the right of a ship or aircraft

stealth
Secretive and avoiding notice

supercharger
A pump that helps an engine take in more air and so in turn burn more fuel

suspension
A system of shock absorbers and springs that cushions the vibrations sent from a road surface to a vehicle

tender
A railroad car that carries fuel and water as part of a steam train

thrust
The force produced by a jet or rocket engine that sends it forward

INDEX